Quilts, Rag Dolls, and Rocking Chairs

Folk Arts and Crafts

D1529496

North American Folklore for Youth

Quilts, Rag Dolls, and Rocking Chairs

Folk Arts and Crafts

Gus Snedeker

Mason Crest

Mason Crest
370 Reed Road
Broomall, Pennsylvania 19008
www.masoncrest.com

First printing
9 8 7 6 5 4 3 2 1

Library of Congress Cataloging-in-Publication Data

Snedeker, Gus.
  Quilts, rag dolls, and rocking chairs : folk arts and crafts / Gus Snedeker.
       p. cm. — (North American folklore for youth)
  Includes index.
  ISBN 978-1-4222-2490-8 (hardcover) — ISBN 978-1-4222-2486-1
(hardcover series) — ISBN 978-1-4222-9255-6 (ebook)
  1. Folk art—North America—Juvenile literature. 2. Handicrafts—North America—Juvenile literature. I. Title.
  NK803.S64 2013
  745.0973—dc23
                                   2012013555

Produced by Harding House Publishing Services, Inc.
www.hardinghousepages.com
Cover design by Torque Advertising + Design.

Contents

Introduction

by Dr. Alan Jabbour

What do a story, a joke, a fiddle tune, a quilt, a dance, a game of jacks, a holiday celebration, and a Halloween costume have in common? Not much, at first glance. But they're all part of the stuff we call "folklore."

The word "folklore" means the ways of thinking and acting that are learned and passed along by ordinary people. Folklore goes from grandparents to parents to children—and on to *their* children. It may be passed along in words, like the urban legend we hear from friends who promise us that it *really* happened to someone they know. Or it may be tunes or dance steps we pick up on the block where we live. It could be the quilt our aunt made. Much of the time we learn folklore without even knowing where or how we learned it.

Folklore is not something that's far away or long ago. It's something we use and enjoy every day! It is often ordinary—

and yet at the same time, it makes life seem very special. Folklore is the culture we share with others in our homes, our neighborhoods, and our places of worship. It helps tell us who we are.

Our first sense of who we are comes from our families. Family folklore—like eating certain meals together or prayers or songs—gives us a sense of belonging. But as we grow older we learn to belong to other groups as well. Maybe your family is Irish. Or maybe you live in a Hispanic neighborhood in New York City. Or you might live in the country in the middle of Iowa. Maybe you're a Catholic—or a Muslim—or you're Jewish. Each one of these groups to which you belong will have it's own folklore. A certain dance step may be African American. A story may have come from Germany. A hymn may be Protestant. A recipe may have been handed down by your Italian grandmother. All this folklore helps the people who belong to a certain group feel connected to each other.

Folklore can make each group special, different from all the others. But at the same time folklore is one of the best ways we can get to know to each other. We can learn about Vietnamese immigrants by eating Vietnamese foods. We can understand newcomers from Somalia by enjoying their music and dance. Stories, songs, and artwork move from group to group. And everyone is the richer!

Folklore isn't something you usually learn in school. Somebody, somewhere, taught you that jump-rope rhyme you know—but you probably can't remember *who* taught you. You definitely didn't learn it in a schoolbook, though! You can study folklore and learn about it—that's what you are doing now in this book!—but folklore normally is something that just gets passed along from person to person.

This series of books explores the many kinds folklore you can find across the North American continent. As you read, you'll learn something about yourself—and you'll learn about your neighbors as well!

ONE
Useful Art

What do you think of when you think of the word "art"? Paintings? Sculptures? Music or dance?

All of these things can be called art. Paintings, sculptures, and music are all nice things. They're beautiful. They make us feel good. Or maybe they make us think.

But other kinds of art are not just pretty to look at. And they don't just make us think. They're also useful objects. Jewelry can be art, for example, even though we wear it. Baskets can be art, even though we use them to carry things.

All of these useful things are also beautiful. They might make us think. So they're art. But we also use them for something.

Folk art is made because people need it to do a job. Folk art includes quilts, baskets, soap, bowls, and many other things. Ordinary people made folk art—and still do today! You don't have to be a *professional* artist to make folk art.

Today we don't make most of the things we use. We buy them in stores. But your great-grandparents probably made lots of the things they used. And your great-great-grandparents may have made almost all the things they needed.

Think about the things you use every day. Things like plastic bags, for example. A hundred years ago, people didn't have

Pottery is another useful art. Most North American Native pottery is made from clay that people dug out of the ground. Native people made their pottery in shapes that were useful for carrying things like water or berries. Water jugs were shaped with narrow tops so that the water did not spill as it was carried from streams. Chamber pots were also made from clay. They were used as toilets during the night and then emptied and cleaned each morning.

The glazes and symbols used to decorate the pottery made it beautiful. Some Native Americans used symbols like deer, eagles, and trees. For other potters, simple designs made with sponges and combs created a nice effect.

plastic bags. But they still needed to carry things. They needed something for carrying things like fruit and vegetables or other small objects. So instead of using plastic bags, they often used baskets woven from some sort of plant material. Those baskets were made by hand. And two hundred years ago, people didn't go to the store to buy a basket. They made it themselves.

When black Americans used to work on plantations as slaves, they needed big baskets to carry grain, cotton, or fish. Men made the big baskets. They used plants called rushes. Women needed smaller baskets for inside. They made them from grasses.

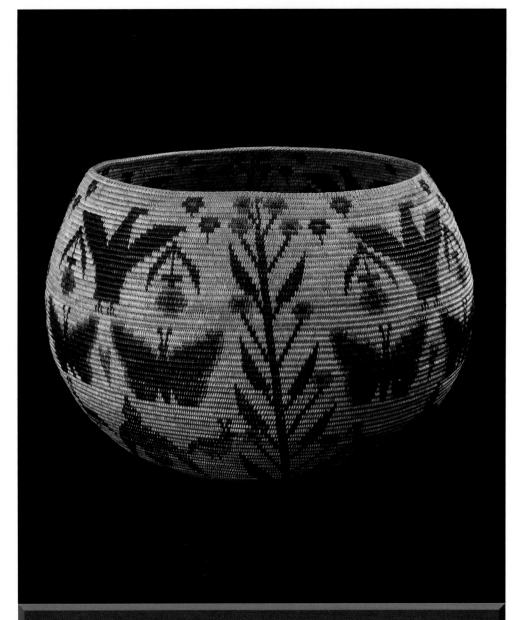

Native baskets are very beautiful, and the people who make them are skilled craftspeople. This basket was made by a Paiute basketmaker from California.

Native people also made baskets. They used them to carry babies, food, and seeds. Baskets were made from grasses, roots, and shrubs.

In the Appalachian Mountains, people made baskets too. They used small pieces of oak wood and willow trees. They wove this wood together to make their baskets.

All these baskets are today thought of as folk art. The people who made them wanted them to be useful. They also wanted them to look nice. They used different colored materials to create patterns. Sometimes they drew pictures on them. They were useful *and* decorative.

But the ordinary people who made these things didn't think of themselves as artists. They were just making things they needed. Making things was just part of a normal day for them.

✳ TWO
Furniture:
A Place to Rest

Think about the furniture in your room. Your bed, dresser, and desk probably all came from a store. Or maybe your parents bought them at a garage sale.

If you were living a hundred years ago, though, your parents would have probably made your furniture. You might have even helped.

Without furniture, a house or apartment would be pretty empty! Furniture gives us a place to rest. It also gives us a place to keep things.

Think about the story of Goldilocks and the Three Bears. Remember how important it was for Goldilocks to find the right-sized chair? And how she needed a bed that was soft enough for her to fall asleep? Having comfortable furniture is important! Chairs have to be the right size and strong enough to hold the people that sit on them. If they're not, they'll be uncomfortable. They might break when someone sits on them! Beds have to be comfortable, so we can fall asleep.

The Amish people still make by hand many of the things they need. This wooden rocking chair is an example of Amish folk art.

This rustic bed is an example of folk art typical of the Appalachian Mountains.

Furniture makers knew this. They knew they had to make chairs, drawers, beds, and other things that would be strong and comfortable. They also wanted to make things that people liked to look at.

What furniture looked like depended on what materials were around. Different furniture makers used different kinds of wood. If you lived near oak trees, you would make furniture from oak wood. If you lived near maple trees, you would make furniture from maple wood. Each wood looks a little different.

This wardrobe was handmade and then hand painted, which makes it a good example of folk art.

Some furniture makers only made one type of furniture. They got really good at making rocking chairs. Or cupboards. They had special designs for them. Each one was unique because it was handmade.

Not all furniture is made in factories today. There are still people who make furniture by hand. You can find handmade furniture at arts-and-crafts stores. Some furniture makers have special stores you can visit. Handmade furniture is usually pretty expensive. That's because it takes a long time to make something by hand.

# THREE
Folk Toys

> **Words to Understand**
>
> *Ceremonies* are sets of acts performed the same way over and over to celebrate an important event.
>
> *Creativity* is the ability to make something new and beautiful or to come up with new ideas.

K ids around the world have loved toys for a long time. Toys are a part of growing up. And toys have been made for thousands of years.

Historians don't know for sure if the first toys were made for kids, though. Some think that objects (like a doll) were given to kids when they weren't needed anymore for religious *ceremonies*. Slowly dolls and other toys were specifically made for kids.

Early toys were made out of whatever materials were around. Dried gourds were filled with seeds—and they became rattles. Old fabric, cornhusks, or leather was made into dolls.

That's common in all folk art. Ordinary people made things from whatever they had handy. They turned available material into useful

Folk art dolls made from yarn and felt.

and fun things for the whole family. They weren't as fancy as the toys you find at stores today. They were much simpler— but just as fun for kids back then.

Dolls might have been a piece of cloth rolled up and tied in the top, middle, and bottom. A face and hair would be added. Then kids could play house or go on adventures with their ragdolls.

Dolls looked like the people that made them. Native American dolls looked like the tribes they came from. They had feathers or fur. They had beads sewn on or ribbons attached to them.

Some people made wooden dolls. They were hand-carved to look like people. Then they were painted and dressed in clothes.

Noah's Ark used to be a popular toy. The toy represented the Bible story of Noah and the flood. It was a boat with pairs of lots of different kinds of animals. Some Arks were made from wood. Others were made of clay or cloth. Some were painted or had moving parts like doors or wheels. Noah's Arks were a way to teach children about religion. Most kids didn't like sitting still in church for hours at a time. It was hard to pay

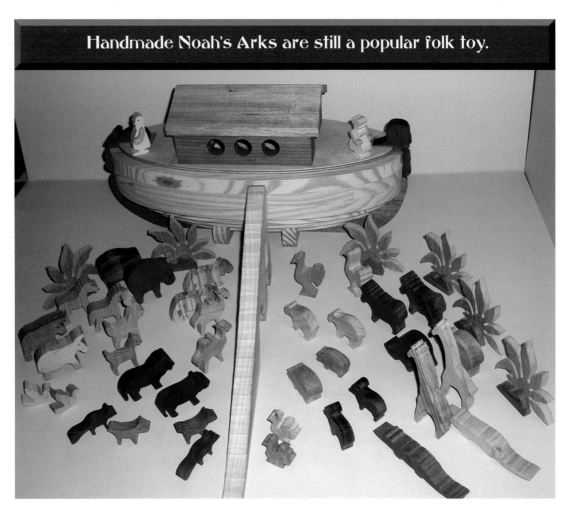

Handmade Noah's Arks are still a popular folk toy.

The dreidel is a top made of four sides, used in a game associated with the Jewish holiday of Hanukkah. Nowadays, it's considered a kid's toy. But legend says that adults first made dreidels as reminders of their faith. At the time Jews were forbidden to meet and study their religion. They carried a dreidel with them instead. When soldiers approached, they could pretend to be playing a game instead of studying religion.

Dreidels are a type of folk toy that have come to be associated with the Jewish holiday of Hannukah.

attention. But they could learn the story of Noah's Ark while they played.

Spinning tops were another popular folk toy. The very first tops were from nature. Kids would pick up an acorn and spin it around. Later, people carved tops from wood.

Across North America, toys have always been important parts of kids' lives. Playing teaches lessons about sharing and getting along. Kids use *creativity* when they play. The parents who made the toys were also creating a kind of folk art.

✳ FOUR
Religious Folk Art

Religious folk art is one way that people make their faith strong. They make things that will remind them of their beliefs.

Religious folk art used to be very important before most people could read or write. People couldn't read about their religion—but they could look at art.

Most religious folk art in North America has to do with Christianity. Most of the European settlers who came to the

United States and Canada were Christians. They believed in God and Jesus. They thought the Bible was important. They went to church.

Folk art helps tell the stories of the Bible. Pictures and sculptures can tell these stories.

Crosses are one sort of religious folk art. Crosses make people think of Jesus and his death and rebirth. People carved crosses for their own homes or for churches. Sometimes they painted them. Or they wove them from grasses.

TRADITIONAL EASTER EGGS

Today, many people make Easter eggs using kits they buy from a store. But in the old days, only colors found in nature were used. You can still use natural options:

- Straw and saffron produce yellow-colored eggs.
- Red beets or plums create red.
- Grass, moss, or spinach make green.
- Blackberries make purple.
- Sunflower seeds produce blue.
- Coffee makes brown.
- Walnut shells create black.

Hispanic Christians are very fond of the Virgin Mary, the mother of Jesus. The Virgin Mary is everywhere. There are paintings of her on walls, on playing cards, and even on air fresheners. She's a very popular folk art *icon*.

Christian folk art is still around today. Do you ever decorate Easter eggs? Or made a Christmas tree ornament? Those are both a kind of folk art!

Folk artists make very fancy and beautiful Easter eggs. These were made in the Czech Republic using straw to make patterns on the dyed eggs.

A tankha is a painting that represents Buddha and his teachings. Teachers of Buddhism used these pictures to spread their beliefs. The technique for making the tankha is spiritual and symbolic. The colors used to paint the pictures are all made from natural dyes from vegetables.

SANTEROS

In the Southwest, people called *santeros* would travel from village to village. They carried wood carving tools with them on their donkeys. They carved sculptures of Christian saints.

The santeros used whatever materials they found. Then they would carve trees and roots into a village's favorite saint. They painted them. Then they sold them to the villagers. And then they moved on to the next village.

Jewish people have their own folk art. For example, Jewish families use menorahs to celebrate Hannukah, the celebration of light. Many North American Jews have crafted their own menorahs. They are made from wood, clay, or metal. Some menorahs have been handed down from **generation** to generation. Kids today sometimes even make menorahs in school.

All these things are examples of folk art. People made these things to remind them of their faith. Today, though, lots of people like to look at these things just because they are beautiful.

✳ FIVE
Folk Instruments

Once there was an old donkey who had worked hard for his master. Now he was old and could not carry heavy loads any more. Knowing that his master would get rid of him if he were of no use, the donkey decided to become a musician.

As he walked along the road, he came upon a dog who was lying in the dirt panting.

"Why are you panting like that?" the donkey asked.

"I am old and cannot hunt any longer," the dog said. "My master wants to kill me so I have run away. I don't know what to do."

"Well, dog, I have the answer," the donkey said. "Come with me and we will be musicians together."

So the two musicians walked further down the road until they came upon a cat. She was very sad.

"Why are you so sad?" the donkey asked.

"I am in danger," the cat said. "Because I am old and no longer chase mice, my mistress wants to drown me. I don't know how I will survive."

"Well," the donkey said, "come with us. We are going to be musicians."

So the three continued down the road until they came to a rooster who was sitting on a fence, crowing as loud as he could.

"Those are some loud cries," said the donkey. "What is wrong?"

"My mistress has decided to cook me for dinner on Sunday because she is getting company."

"Oh, dear," said the donkey. "Why don't you come with us to become a musician?"

So all four went on their way until dark, when they decided to rest in the woods. The rooster climbed a tree and saw a house in the distance, which he pointed out to the others.

"It is very uncomfortable here. Let's go see if we can find somewhere better to sleep in that house."

When they arrived, they realized the house belonged to robbers. So the musicians devised a plan to scare them off. The donkey put his forefeet on the windowsill, the dog climbed to the donkey's back, the cat on the dog's back, and finally the rooster onto the cat's back. When a signal was given, they all began to perform their music. The sound burst into the room inside.

The robbers jumped up from the food-laden table and ran into the woods in terror. The four musicians feasted on a good meal and went to sleep—the donkey outside, the dog behind

The story of the animal musicians is a famous folktale called "The Musicians of Bremen," which has inspired folk art like this.

the door, the cat on the hearth by the warm ashes, and the cock on a roof rafter.

Not wanting to be pushed out of their house, the robbers came up with a plan. They sent one robber back to the house to find out what had happened. But when he went into the kitchen and struck a match for light, he scared the cat who flew into his face, spitting and scratching. He ran to the backdoor where the dog bit his leg. As he rushed outside, the donkey kicked him and the cock awakened with a loud cry.

The robber returned to his captain saying, "There is a witch with long nails in the kitchen, and a man with a knife at the door. In the yard is a large monster with a club and on the roof sits someone yelling for justice." So the robbers left and never came back. And the four musicians stayed right where they were.

This folktale tells about the power of music. The four animals in the story didn't have very happy lives. When they decided to become musicians, suddenly their futures were very bright!

In the past, people had to work very hard. They used music to relax and have fun. (We still do this today.) Music can bring people together. It gives them hope. It makes them happy.

Of course, to make music, you either need to sing or play an instrument. Many folk artists made their own instruments to play music.

Native Americans made lots of instruments. Most of them were used for religious ceremonies. Drums were especially important. They kept the beat while people danced and sang.

Later European settlers made their own instruments. In the Appalachian Mountains, people played an instrument called the dulcimer. It's kind of like a harp you play on your lap. Dulcimers are made from wood. They have designs on the front.

Many folk musicians made fiddles (or violins). They carved designs into the wood with knives.

Another folk instrument is the tin whistle, or pennywhistle. It's a simple instrument like a flute. It's easy to make from wood or bone, and easy to play.

The fife is a similar instrument. Fifes were important folk instruments during the Revolutionary War. When the colonists were marching to war, a fife player would play a marching tune.

In the days before mp3 players and computers, people had to rely on making music themselves. They had to make their own drums, fiddles, and whistles if they wanted music!

 # SIX
Cloth Arts

Fabric is important to our lives. Think about it. We use fabric to keep us warm. We make clothes and blankets from it. We use it for cleaning our homes. We also use it for decoration.

Clothing

Today, you can buy your clothes at the store. A long time ago, though, there weren't any clothing stores. Women made their families' clothes and blankets.

One way they made clothes was by knitting. They used yarn and a couple of big knitting needles to create woven socks. They also knit sweaters, blankets, mittens, and hats. Lots of people still knit today. Maybe you know someone who does—or maybe you yourself know how to knit.

People sometimes even made their own cloth for clothes. It was a long process. First, they needed wool from a sheep. They untangled the wool using two big brushes. Then they died the wool. They used different plants to make the dyes. Next they made it into thread using a spinning wheel. Then they wove the thread on a big machine called a loom. Making fabric took a lot of work and many days.

Bedcovers

Bedcovers might be made from woven fabric, but another way that people made bedcovers was by quilting. Quilts are made from lots and lots of different pieces of cloth sewn together in layers. The top layer is made from pieces of cloth cut in shapes like triangles and squares, sewn together into a pattern. Women (and a few men) have been making quilts for a long time.

Making quilts together was once a chance for women to get together and talk. They all worked on a quilt together. They got to have a good time with their friends. And they finished a beautiful quilt that would keep someone warm. These gatherings were called quilting bees.

Today, quilting is still a popular folk craft. Many people still make quilts. They make quilts to cover beds. And they make quilts because they're beautiful.

DID YOU KNOW?

Two hundred years ago in North America, some children learned to knit and crochet caps and mittens when they were as young as six years old!

In the 1700s and 1800s, little girls made "samplers" like this to help them learn how to embroider different stitches.

Rugs

People have always wanted rugs to keep their feet warm. One kind of cloth folk art is hooked rugs.

Small pieces of cloth from old clothes were used to make hooked rugs. The folk artist drew a picture or design on a piece of cloth. Then really thin pieces of fabric were pulled up through the back of the cloth in loops. When the rug was done, the tiny fabric loops made a design.

Some rugs were made from braided strips of old cloth. Tablemats and other flat things could be made this way too.

Using old clothes to make rugs was a way to *recycle* fabric. It meant that nothing was wasted or thrown away. And at the same time, something beautiful was created.

Decoration

Some fabric folk art was more for decoration. Lots of women learned how to embroider. They covered fabric with detailed pictures using just a needle and thread.

Women covered pillows, blankets, and wall hangings with embroidery. It made the home a little prettier. Embroidery also decorated clothing

Many of the designs used in traditional folk art are still used today. And plenty of people still enjoy these folk arts. Quilting, furniture making, knitting, and instrument making are all still practiced today.

Find Out More

In Books

Kafka, Tina. *Folk Art.* Farmington Hills, Mich.: Lucent, 2007.

Michaels, Alexandra. *The Kids Multicultural Art Book: Art and Craft Experiences from Around the World.* Danbury, Conn.: Williamson, 2007.

Panchyk, Richard. *American Folk Art for Kids.* Chicago: Chicago Review Press, 2004.

Polacco, Patricia. *The Keeping Quilt.* Fullerton, Calif.: Aladdin, 2001.

On the Internet

How to Make a Rag Doll
crafts-for-kids.craftideasweekly.com/make-easy-rag-doll

Quilting Bees
www.womenfolk.com/quilting_history/quilting.htm

Underground Railroad Quilts
www.osblackhistory.com/quilts.php

Index

Picture Credits

About the Author and the Consultant

Gus Snedeker is proud of his heritage as a Dutch American. He loves to study the stories and traditions of the various groups of people who helped build America. He has also written several other books in this series.

Dr. Alan Jabbour is a folklorist who served as the founding director of the American Folklife Center at the Library of Congress from 1976 to 1999. Previously, he began the grant-giving program in folk arts at the National Endowment for the Arts (1974-76). A native of Jacksonville, Florida, he was trained at the University of Miami (B.A.) and Duke University (M.A., Ph.D.). A violinist from childhood on, he documented old-time fiddling in the Upper South in the 1960s and 1970s. A specialist in instrumental folk music, he is known as a fiddler himself, an art he acquired directly from elderly fiddlers in North Carolina, Virginia, and West Virginia. He has taught folklore and folk music at UCLA and the University of Maryland and has published widely in the field.